Volcanoes

D0033948

Wendy Pirk

What is a Volcano?

A **volcano** is a hole in the earth's crust where molten rock and gases from the earth's core escape to the surface.

The word "volcano" comes from Vulcan, the Roman god of fire and metalworking.

Vulcan was the blacksmith of the gods. The ancient Romans believed he lived under the volcano on Vulcano, an island off the coast of Sicily.

They thought any noise, ash and lava that came from Vulcano was caused by Vulcan creating weapons and lightning bolts for the gods.

The earth is made up of four main layers: the crust, the mantle, the outer core and the inner core.

The crust is the hard surface we walk on and where all things grow. It is like the eggshell surrounding an egg.

The mantle is more than 45 times thicker than the crust. Here the hot magma is thick and gooey, like melted cheese.

The outer core is made up of mostly iron and nickel. It is so hot that the minerals are liquid.

The inner core is solid iron. The pressure from the outer core, mantle and crust pushing on it keeps it from melting.

In some places in the ocean the crust is quite thin, about as deep as 20 soccer fields are long. In other places, like under mountains, it can be as thick as 650 soccer fields.

The Earth's Layers

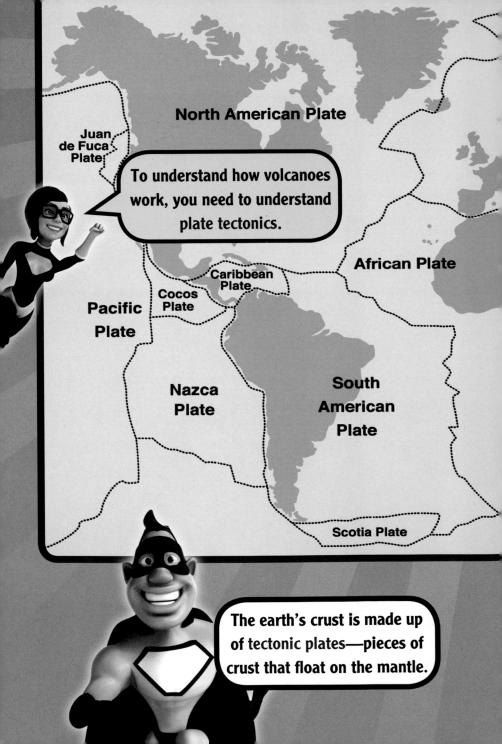

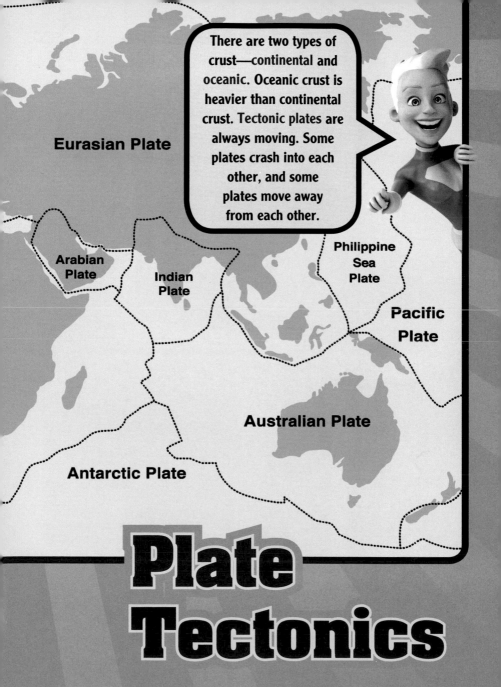

There are two types of crust—continental and oceanic. Oceanic crust is heavier than continental crust. Tectonic plates are always moving. Some plates crash into each other, and some plates move away from each other.

Eurasian Plate

Arabian Plate

Indian Plate

Philippine Sea Plate

Pacific Plate

Australian Plate

Antarctic Plate

Plate Tectonics

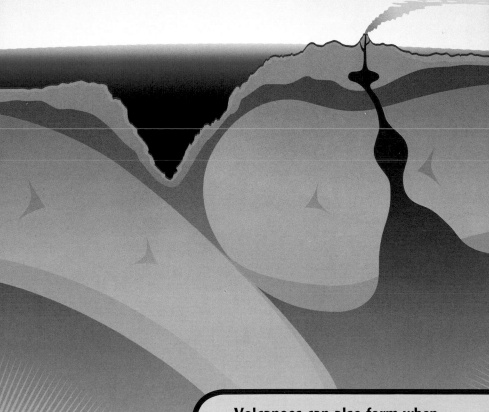

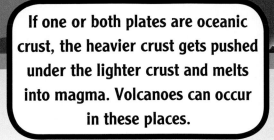

If one or both plates are oceanic crust, the heavier crust gets pushed under the lighter crust and melts into magma. Volcanoes can occur in these places.

Volcanoes can also form when magma breaks through a weak spot in a tectonic plate and pushes up to the surface. These places are called hot spots.

The Ring of Fire is an area of the Pacific Ocean where the Pacific plate pushes against the plates around it. It is called the Ring of Fire because so many volcanoes are found there.

R I N G   O F

Aleutian trench

Kurile trench

Japan trench

Izu Ogasawara trench

Ryukyu trench

Philippine trench

Mt. Pinatubo

Mt. Mayon

Marianas trench

Challenger Deep

Equator

Bougainville trench

Krakatoa

Java (Sunda) trench

Tonga trench

Kermadec trench

Indonesia has 147 volcanoes, more than any other country. Seventy-six of these volcanoes are active.

Mt. Garibaldi
Mt. St. Helens

The Ring of Fire has 75 percent of the world's active volcanoes.

F I R E

Puerto Rico trench

Middle America trench

Peru-Chile trench

South Sandwich trench

Ring of Fire

The Parts of a Volcano

Fumarole: a type of vent where steam and gases escape into the air.

Crater: a bowl-shaped basin around a volcanic vent where the magma, ash and gases escape. It is usually at the top of a volcano. A caldera is a type of crater that is formed when the top of a volcano collapses.

There are three main types of volcanoes:

- composite volcanoes
- shield volcanoes
- cinder cones.

Types of Volcanoes

Composite volcanoes are large, steep-sided volcanoes built from layers of lava covered by layers of ash and rock. They are also known as stratovolcanos.

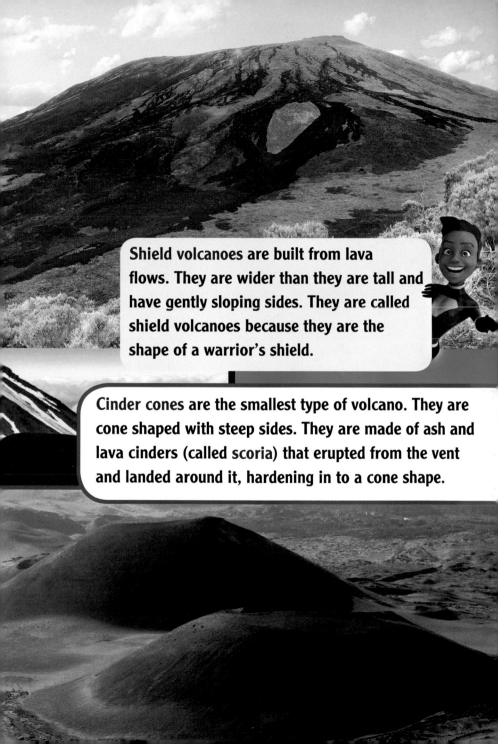

Shield volcanoes are built from lava flows. They are wider than they are tall and have gently sloping sides. They are called shield volcanoes because they are the shape of a warrior's shield.

Cinder cones are the smallest type of volcano. They are cone shaped with steep sides. They are made of ash and lava cinders (called scoria) that erupted from the vent and landed around it, hardening in to a cone shape.

Submarine volcanoes grow underwater around vents on the ocean floor. These volcanoes are more active than volcanoes on land.

Hawaii

Submarine volcanoes can form underwater mountains. If these mountains get big enough, they break through the ocean's surface and become volcanic islands.

Iceland

Iceland and Hawaii are volcanic islands.

Submarine Volcanoes

A dormant volcano has not erupted or shown any activity in the last 10,000 years, but it could erupt sometime in the future.

An extinct volcano is one that is not expected to erupt again. There is no sure way to know when a volcano might erupt. Even volcanoes thought to be extinct have erupted.

Types of Eruption

There are two main types of volcanic eruptions, effusive and explosive. In an effusive eruption, the lava is runny and flows like syrup down the side of the volcano.

In an explosive eruption, the lava is thick. Volcanic gases get trapped in the magma, and pressure builds up until the volcano finally explodes. Picture what happens when you shake a can of pop and then open it. Boom! That's what happens in an explosive eruption.

Explo-ive Eruptions

There are 4 main types of explosive eruption: Strombolian, Pelean, Vulcanian and Plinian.

STROMBOLIAN ERUPTION

PELEAN ERUPTION

In a Strombolian eruption, lava shoots out of the volcano in many small explosions. These eruptions are usually one of the least dangerous types.

Pelean eruptions happen when a lava dome collapses. They are known for pyroclastic flows.

Vulcanian eruptions are more violent. They happen when a lava dome or lava plug explodes. These eruptions create huge clouds of ash, small pieces of rock and sometimes pyroclastic flows.

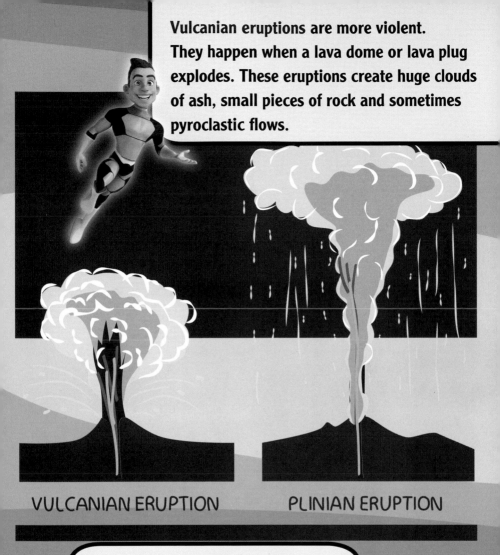

VULCANIAN ERUPTION   PLINIAN ERUPTION

The biggest, most violent type of eruption is the Plinian eruption. It usually happens with composite volcanoes. The eruption plume can reach twice as high as a plane can fly. Huge rocks and ash can be thrown far away from the volcano.

Explosions!

Scientists use this Volcanic Explosivity Index (VEI) to rate how strong an eruption is. The scale goes from 1 to 8. Each number on the scale is 10 times more explosive than the number before it (for example 7, is 10 times more explosive than 6).

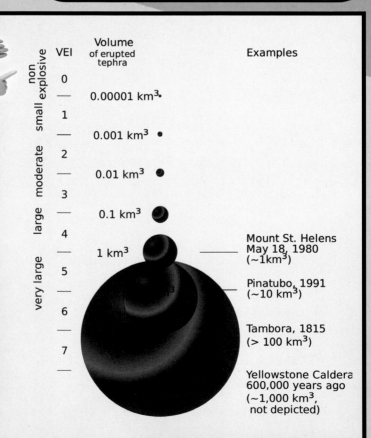

	VEI	Volume of erupted tephra		Examples
non explosive	0			
small	1	0.00001 km³		
	2	0.001 km³		
moderate	3	0.01 km³		
large	4	0.1 km³		
very large	5	1 km³		Mount St. Helens May 18, 1980 (~1km³)
	6			Pinatubo, 1991 (~10 km³)
	7			Tambora, 1815 (> 100 km³)
				Yellowstone Caldera 600,000 years ago (~1,000 km³, not depicted)

Supervolcanoes

A supervolcano is one that erupts with a force thousands of times stronger than a regular volcano. Rather than being a mountain or hill, a supervolcano is a usually a pit in the ground.

A supervolcano forms when magma from a hotspot cannot make its way to the surface and pools into a huge magma chamber under the crust. When the pressure gets too strong, the crust explodes, leaving behind a giant caldera. These calderas are so big they can be seen from space.

Types of Lava

When a volcano is erupting, the lava can move slowly, like honey, or as quickly as a car on the highway, depending on the type. There are three main types of lava: a'a, pahoehoe and pillow.

A'a lava is thick and clumpy. Huge chunky blocks ooze down the side of the volcano as though they are being pushed from behind.

Pahoehoe lava is thin and runny. It flows smoothly down the side of the volcano. The surface of the lava cools into a crust as the air touches it. Hot lava still flows under the crust.

When hot lava flows beneath a cooled lava crust, it forms a lava tube. Once the eruption ends and the lava stops flowing, the tube becomes an underground tunnel.

Pit craters form when magma pools under the Earth's crust, because it can't crack through to the surface. It drains back into the magma chamber leaving behind a hole. Once the magma is gone, the ground above the hole collapses, forming a pit.

Volcanic Dangers

Volcanoes can be really destructive. There is no way to stop flowing lava. It can bury everything in its path. Many people have tried to change the direction the lava flows, but it usually doesn't work.

In 1669, the people of Catania, Italy, tried digging trenches to direct flowing lava away from their town. If the trenches had worked, the lava would have gone toward the nearby town of Paterno. That did not please Paterno's townsfolk. The people of the two towns fought, and the Catanians had to stop building their trenches. In the end, the lava destroyed half of Catania.

People have also tried bombing lava tubes, building high barriers and cooling the lava with seawater.

AREA CLOSED
ACTIVE LAVA FLOW
**EXTREMELY
HAZARDOUS**
NO ACCESS ALLOWED

VIOLATORS WILL BE SUBJECT TO
CIVIL FINES AND/OR CRIMINAL
PROSECUTION.

ORITY HRS §171-6 AND HAR §13-221-4

STATE of HAWAII
DEPARTMENT of LAND and
NATURAL RESOURCES

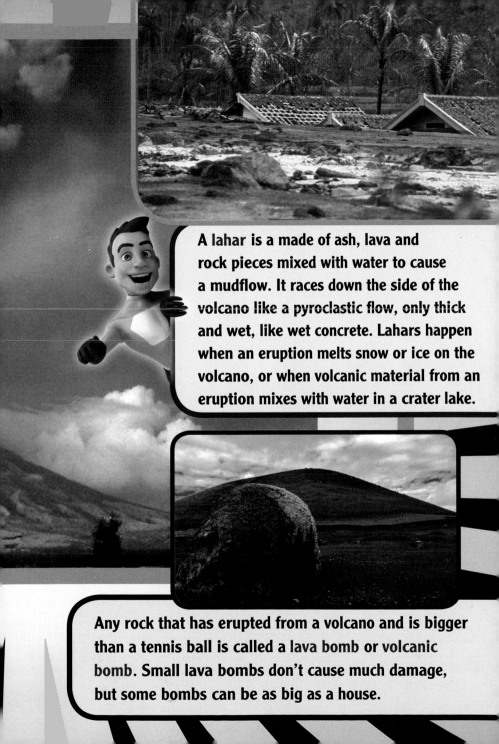

A lahar is a made of ash, lava and rock pieces mixed with water to cause a mudflow. It races down the side of the volcano like a pyroclastic flow, only thick and wet, like wet concrete. Lahars happen when an eruption melts snow or ice on the volcano, or when volcanic material from an eruption mixes with water in a crater lake.

Any rock that has erupted from a volcano and is bigger than a tennis ball is called a lava bomb or volcanic bomb. Small lava bombs don't cause much damage, but some bombs can be as big as a house.

Volcanic Ash

Volcanic ash is made up of tiny pieces of sharp rock, volcanic glass and minerals. People who breathe it in can develop lung disease. If it gets into someone's eyes, it can scratch the eyeball.

Volcanic ash is another dangerous effect of volcanic eruptions. Thick layers of ash can kill plants, destroy people's homes and bury roads.

In April 2010, Iceland's Eyjafjallajökull* volcano erupted and sent a huge ash cloud into the atmosphere. The ash cloud stopped all airline flights in many countries in Europe and North America for more than a week. Some countries had to cancel flights even into the first half of May because wind pushed the ash cloud through their airspace.

* We don't know how to pronounce this name either!

Mount St. Helens

Mount St. Helens is one of the most active volcanoes in the United States. On May 18, 1980, the volcano erupted, but not from its peak. It erupted from a vent on its side. The force of the eruption blew off most of the north side of the volcano.

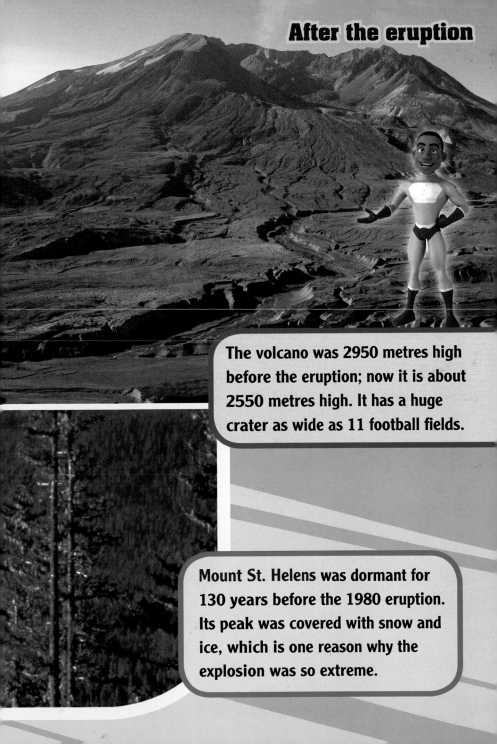

The volcano was 2950 metres high before the eruption; now it is about 2550 metres high. It has a huge crater as wide as 11 football fields.

Mount St. Helens was dormant for 130 years before the 1980 eruption. Its peak was covered with snow and ice, which is one reason why the explosion was so extreme.

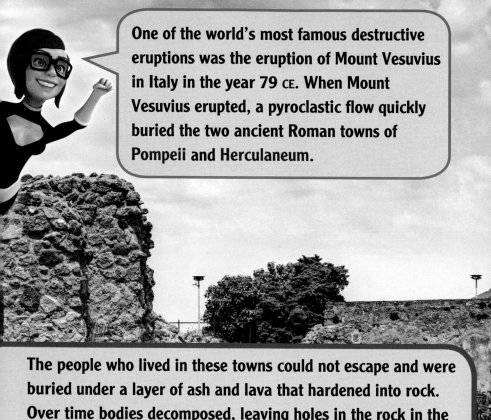

One of the world's most famous destructive eruptions was the eruption of Mount Vesuvius in Italy in the year 79 CE. When Mount Vesuvius erupted, a pyroclastic flow quickly buried the two ancient Roman towns of Pompeii and Herculaneum.

The people who lived in these towns could not escape and were buried under a layer of ash and lava that hardened into rock. Over time bodies decomposed, leaving holes in the rock in the shape of the body that once lay there. Archaeologists poured plaster into the holes, and when it hardened, they could see what the buried people looked like.

Pompeii

Archaeologists who studied the Pompeii site had to dig through volcanic rock as deep as a 1-storey building before they reached the buried town. The rock covering Herculaneum was 5 times deeper.

Krakatau

Krakatau

Alice Springs

The 1883 eruption of Krakatau is thought to be the loudest sound heard in modern history. The explosion was heard more than 2500 kilometres away in Alice Springs, Australia!

In 1927 a new volcanic island, Anak Krakatau, grew out of the caldera left behind from the 1883 explosion. Its name means "Child of Krakatau."

The Krakatau eruption destroyed the island the volcano was on and caused huge tsunamis with waves higher than a 12-storey building. About 34,000 people died because of the eruption.

Another famous eruption was the 1815 eruption of Mount Tambora in Indonesia. This eruption is the largest eruption in recorded history. It is considered a 7 on the VEI. More than 71,000 people died during this eruption.

When the volcano exploded, it blasted so much ash into the atmosphere that it blocked out the sun for months. The climate became cooler, causing crops to fail. People went hungry throughout Europe, Asia and North America. The year 1816 became known as the "Year Without a Summer."

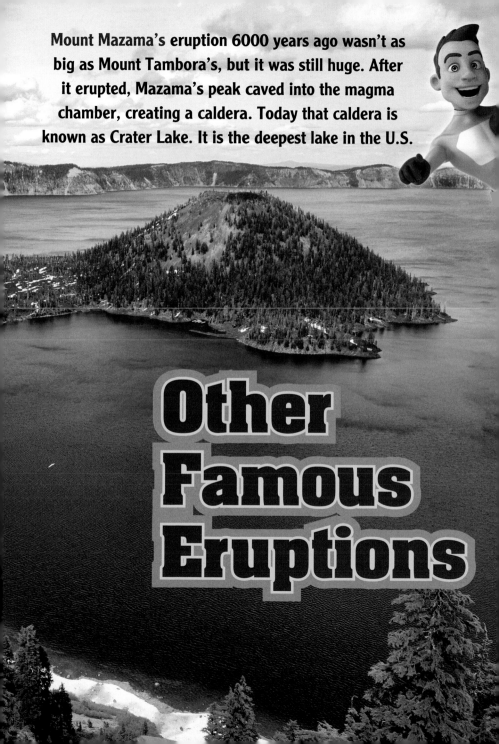

Mount Mazama's eruption 6000 years ago wasn't as big as Mount Tambora's, but it was still huge. After it erupted, Mazama's peak caved into the magma chamber, creating a caldera. Today that caldera is known as Crater Lake. It is the deepest lake in the U.S.

Other Famous Eruptions

Volcanoes may have caused the extinction of the dinosaurs. The ash from volcanic eruptions may have changed the climate so much that the dinosaurs could not survive.

Dinosaur Extinction

Uses of Volcanic Ash

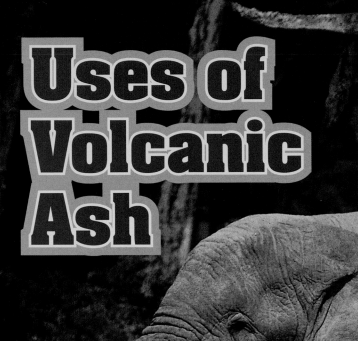

Volcanoes can be destructive, but they can also be helpful. Volcanic ash is rich in minerals. These minerals make the soil rich, which helps plants grow. Many creatures eat plants grown in volcanic soil.

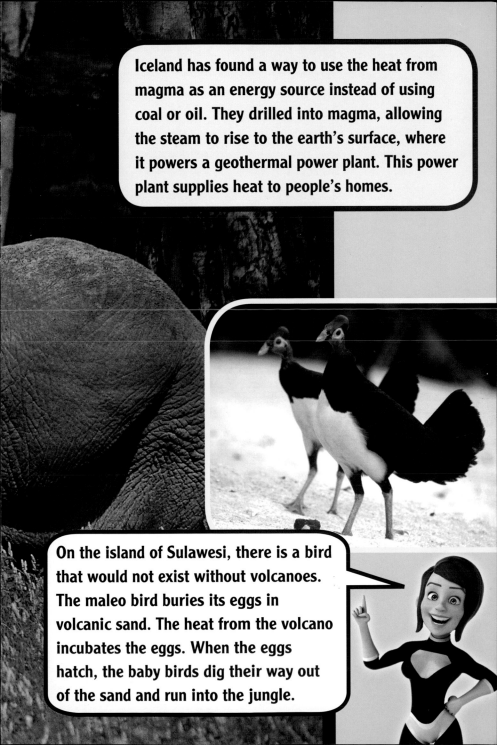

Iceland has found a way to use the heat from magma as an energy source instead of using coal or oil. They drilled into magma, allowing the steam to rise to the earth's surface, where it powers a geothermal power plant. This power plant supplies heat to people's homes.

On the island of Sulawesi, there is a bird that would not exist without volcanoes. The maleo bird buries its eggs in volcanic sand. The heat from the volcano incubates the eggs. When the eggs hatch, the baby birds dig their way out of the sand and run into the jungle.

Even though they watch and study volcanoes, volcanologists still cannot always predict when one might erupt.

Scientists can tell when a volcano is active. Magma moving under and pushing against the crust causes the ground to shake. They use a seismograph to record the movement under the crust. Changes in movement might be a sign that a volcano is going to erupt.

Predicting Eruptions

Other signs researchers watch for are:
• a higher than usual level of sulphur
  dioxide in the volcanic gases
• swelling of the volcanoes sides.

Hot Springs

A hot spring is a pool of groundwater that is heated by volcanic activity under the earth's crust. Some hot springs are nice warm pools where people can soak and relax. Others are hot enough to burn or even kill a person or animal that tries to go into them.

The water in a hot spring has a lot of minerals. Some people believe soaking in it can be good for their health. However, some hot springs have bacteria that can make people sick.

No monkey lives in a colder climate than the Japanese macaque. These smart little monkeys take full advantage of hot springs to keep warm on cold winter days. Japanese macaques are also called "snow monkeys."

Yellowstone National Park is famous for Old Faithful, one of the world's best-known geysers. It erupts about every 75 minutes.

A geyser has a pool of water at the earth's surface and another pool underneath the surface. The water in the underground pool is heated by magma and starts to boil. As the water boils underground, pressure builds and the water is pushed up through vents in the rock. When it reaches the surface pool, the geyser erupts. The eruption ends when the water temperature cools.

Lava that pools in a crater usually either hardens over time or continues to rise until it spills over the edge of the crater. Sometimes the level of lava stays the same but continues to be heated by the magma below. When this happens, a lava lake is formed.

Lava Lakes

Lava lakes are rare. Only five volcanoes in the world have had lava lakes. These volcanoes are in Chile, Antarctica, Ethiopia, the Democratic Republic of Congo and Hawaii.

Erta Ale, a volcano in Ethiopia, Africa, has the oldest lava lake. It formed in the early 1900s and still exists today. The black crust on the lake is a crust of cooled lava.

Acid Lakes

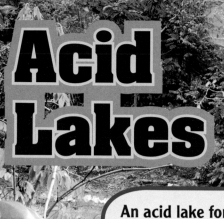

An acid lake forms when volcanic gases leak from the volcano into crater lakes on the top or sides of the volcano.

Mount Ijen's acid lake is the largest, most acidic in the world. The water in the lake is full of sulfur and hydrochloric acid. It can burn your skin if you touch it.

The Publisher: Super Explorers is an imprint of Blue Bike Books

Library and Archives Canada Cataloguing in Publication

Pirk, Wendy, 1973–, author
    Volcanoes / Wendy Pirk.

ISBN 978-1-926700-70-0 (softcover) 978-1-926700-71-7 (e-pub)
    1. Volcanoes—Juvenile literature. I. Title.

QE522.P57 2017   j551.21   C2016-907485-4

Front cover credit: solarseven.

Back cover credits: Vershinin-M, ElenaMirage.

Background graphics: From Thinkstock: cienpies, 20, 21, 34, 35; Igor Zakowski, 8, 9, 12, 13, 14, 15, 16, 17, 22, 23, 26, 27, 33, 50, 51, 54, 55, 60, 61; iwanara-MC, 18, 19, 40, 41; Lana_stem, 30, 31; Nora Vector, 2, 3; shelma1, 38, 39; Yakovliev, 24, 25.

Photo credits: From Thinkstock: abadonian, 19a; Agil_Leonardo, 31a; AliZ59, 39b; Amenohi, 19b; Andre Nantel, p. 34–35; AZ68, 3b, 61; azerberber, 41; bAlllllAd p. 59; bubaone, 46; Byelikova_Oksana, 46–47; DavidByronKeener, 58; DavidSzabo, 13; Digital Vision, 36–37; dodo_dyg, 8–9; doguhakan, 54; DPKuras, 6b; edella, 44; ElenaMirage, 62–63; estivillml, 48–49; etvulc, 25, 32–33; GeorgeBurba, 37; geyzer, 18; Giovanni-Caruso, 4-5, 5; Goce Risteski, 50–51; jchaager, 43; jcthornton, 7b; JochenScheffl, 40–41; Jupiterimages, 6a; kalistratova, 3a; LeeAnnWhite, 17; lucky-photographer, 30–31, 31b; m-kojot, 7a; magcs, 20b; MR 1805, 50; Natalia Moroz, 21; noritos, 57; outcast85, 56–57; PeterHermesFurian, 10–11; Photon-Photos, 35a; picturist, 63; Purestock, 52–53; ronnybuol, 53; Rosario_82, 24; rrvachov, 48; saiko3p, 5; SalvadorGali, 16, 26–27; scaliger, 44–45; shihina, 23; SIYAMA9, 29; solarseven, 22; Stocktrek Images, 20a; strongkrod, 33; Vershinin-M, 54–55, 60–61; warrengoldswain, 40a; yavuzsariyildiz, 61. From Wikipedia: C.G. Newhall, 38–39; chris, 28; Dave Bunnell, 35b; gringer, 14–15; Harry Glicken, USGS/CVO, 42; Marie-Lan Nguyen, 4; Robin Holcomb, 39a.

Superhero illustrations: julos/Thinkstock

Produced with the assistance of the Government of Alberta, Alberta Media Fund.

Alberta ■
Government

We acknowledge the financial support of the Government of Canada.

Funded by the Government of Canada
Financé par le gouvernement du Canada | **Canadä**

PC: 28